THE ULTIMATE ANIMAL LIBRARY

Cheetahs

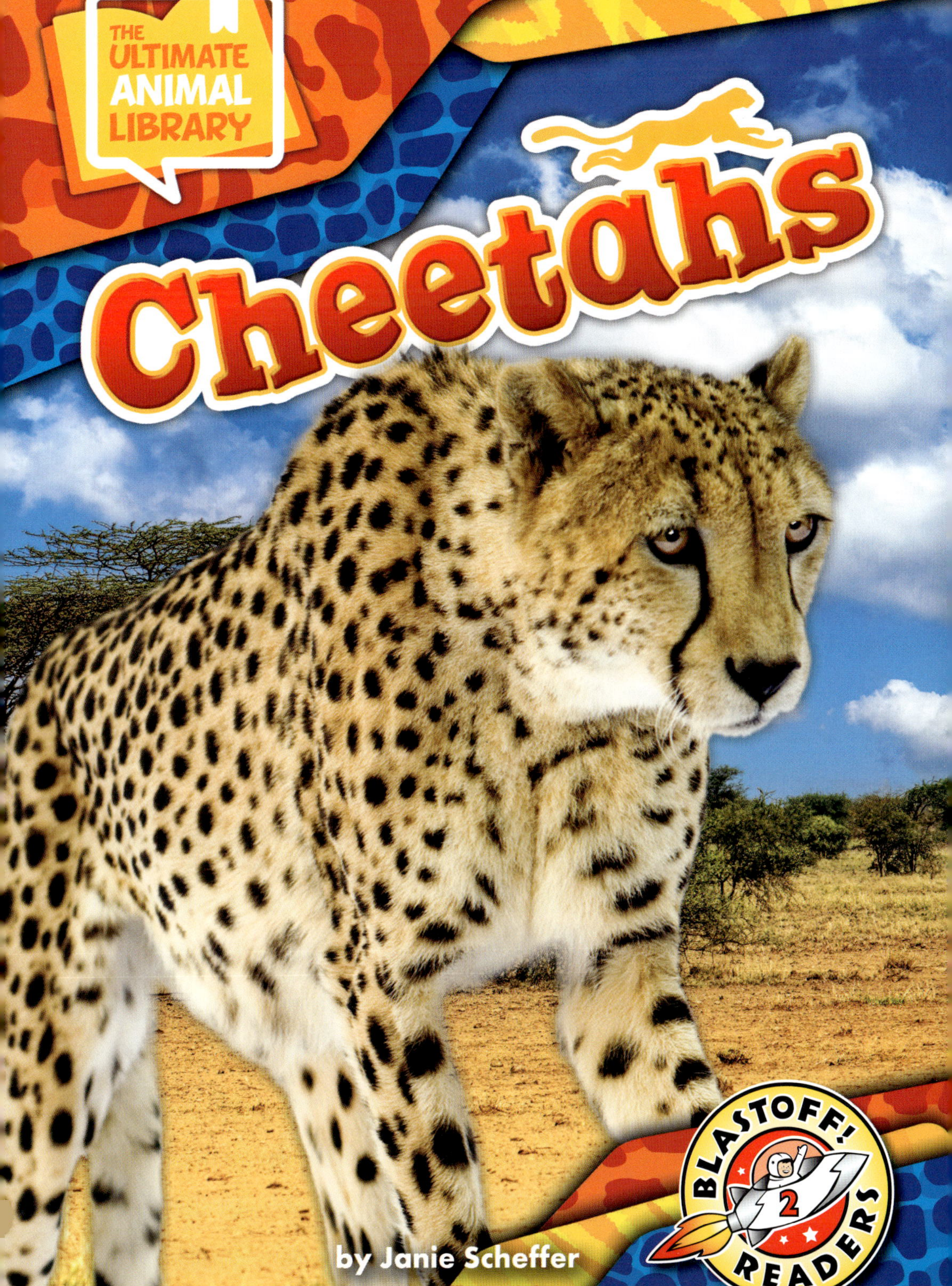

BLASTOFF! READERS 2

by Janie Scheffer

BLASTOFF! READERS, AN IMPRINT OF BELLWETHER MEDIA BY FLUTTERBEE

Blastoff! Readers are carefully developed by literacy experts to build reading stamina and move students toward fluency by combining standards-based content with developmentally appropriate text.

LEVELS

Level 1 provides the most support through repetition of high-frequency words, light text, predictable sentence patterns, and strong visual support.

Level 2 offers early readers a bit more challenge through varied sentences, increased text load, and text-supportive special features.

Level 3 advances early-fluent readers toward fluency through increased text load, less reliance on photos, advancing concepts, longer sentences, and more complex special features.

★ **Blastoff! Universe**

Reading Level

Blastoff! Beginners — Grade K

Blastoff! Readers — Grades 1–3

Blastoff! Discovery — Grade 4

This edition first published in 2027 by Bellwether Media, Inc.

Library of Congress Cataloging-in-Publication Data

Names: Scheffer, Janie, 1992- author
Title: Cheetahs / by Janie Scheffer.
Description: Minneapolis, Minnesota : Bellwether Media, Inc., 2027. | Series: Ultimate animal library | Includes bibliographical references and index. | Audience: Ages 5-8 | Audience: Grades 2-3 | Summary: "Relevant images match informative text in this introduction to cheetahs. Intended for students in kindergarten through third grade"-- Provided by publisher.
Identifiers: LCCN 2026013888 (print) | LCCN 2026013889 (ebook) | ISBN 9798898800406 (library binding) | ISBN 9798898801649 (ebook)
Subjects: LCSH: Cheetah
Classification: LCC QL737.C23 S327 2027 (print) | LCC QL737.C23 (ebook)
LC record available at https://lccn.loc.gov/2026013888
LC ebook record available at https://lccn.loc.gov/2026013889

Editor: Elizabeth Neuenfeldt Designer: Brittany McIntosh

Printed in the United States of America, North Mankato, MN.

Table of Contents

What Are Cheetahs?

Cheetahs are **mammals**. They are the fastest animal on land! They are found in parts of Africa and Iran.

Cheetah Report

Range

Status in the Wild

vulnerable

Habitats

grasslands | savannas | shrublands

Cheetahs have short tan or yellow fur. It is covered with black spots.

They have black tear streaks from their eyes to their mouths.

Cheetahs have thin bodies and long legs. Their backs are **flexible**.

They have hard paw pads and **semi-retractable** claws. These help with **traction** as they run.

Cheetahs have large **nasal passages**. These help them take in more air when they run.

Their eyes are high on their heads. They can see very well!

Spot a Cheetah

Most cheetahs hunt during the day in open **grasslands**.

Their fur helps them hide among grasses. This allows them to **stalk** animals.

Cheetahs must get close to animals they hunt.

These **carnivores** attack gazelles and hares. They eat their meals quickly!

Female cheetahs live alone. Most male cheetahs live in **coalitions**.

Coalitions usually include two or three males. Most are **littermates**.

Growing Up

Female cheetahs give birth to up to eight **cubs** at a time. Cubs are born with dark fur.

They are about 12 inches (30 centimeters) long.

Cubs learn to hunt at six weeks. They leave mom after around a year and a half.

Male littermates stay together. Females go live alone. Cheetahs can live for up to 14 years!

Life of a Cheetah

Name of Babies

cubs

Number of Babies

1 to 8

Time Spent with Mom

around 1 and a half years

Life Span

up to 14 years

Glossary

carnivores—animals that only eat meat

coalitions—groups of male cheetahs

cubs—baby cheetahs

flexible—able to bend

grasslands—lands covered with grasses and other soft plants with few bushes or trees

littermates—groups of baby animals born together at the same time

mammals—warm-blooded animals that have backbones and feed their young milk

nasal passages—the two tunnels inside the nose where air travels when an animal breathes

semi-retractable—able to be partially pulled back in

stalk—to follow closely and quietly

traction—the ability to avoid slipping on a surface while moving